DINNER *for* MARY

A guide to cooking delicious, healthy, real food like I do for my wife.

Ben Ceccarelli

To my wife Mary,

Your hunger for love and life makes me a better man

And your hunger for dinner makes me a better cook.

CONTENTS

ACKNOWLEDGEMENTS

This book would not have been possible without the encouragement and support of so many of my dear friends and family that have been dinner guests and taste-testers over the years.

Thank you Mom for giving me my first ever cooking lesson and for instilling in me the love for a great home-cooked meal. Thank you Dad for always reminding me I can do anything I set my mind to.

Thank you Ian and Rebecca for being my Sunday morning guinea pigs, and testing out all of my creative versions of classic football-watching snacks. Rebecca, without your suggestion on how to publish this book, it may never have gotten started.

Thank you to all of our dinner guests over the years who's happy bellies have given me the drive to continuously work on my cooking craft. Specifically: David & Francesca, Dustin & Stephanie, Doug & Stephen, Jen & Reed, Adrian & Em, MP & Catriona, Finn & July, Jen W, Danielle, Andrea, Bryce & Kristin, and Jeff & Kristina.

Thank you Harry for sparking many culinary epiphanies and for being an honest critic.

Thank you to my many social media followers who have been asking for this book for quite some time. I'm so excited to be able to share this information with all of you.

And of course, thank you Mary. This was all for you.

In 2008, Mary and I took part in a 30-day challenge where we cut out grains, dairy, and processed sugar and focused on eating lean meats, vegetables, and fruit. It was the Paleo Diet challenge, and we went into it hesitant, but with an open mind. We expected to lose some weight, especially by cutting out the grains and sugar, but we had no idea that this 30-day challenge would change our lives forever.

There was a definite uncomfortable adjustment period for the first 10 days or so. Our bodies were trying to get used to this new way of eating, and different source of fuel. After about two weeks, we were both thrilled with the results that were beginning to show. We lost fat, noticeably! I remember walking out of the shower and looking in the mirror, thinking, "I have abs!" Getting lean was amazing, but it was actually just a positive side effect to what was really happening in our bodies. We were finally giving our bodies real food to use as fuel. We slept better, had more energy in the day, and didn't feel bloated or lethargic after a meal. Our workouts improved, our mental focus improved, and we started becoming better versions of ourselves. The meals weren't anything extravagant, but for the 30 days, it was tolerable. What started as a 30-day challenge, soon became our lifestyle.

Mary and I quickly realized that if we were going to make our new eating style work, we were going to have to be better about making meals at home. Eating at restaurants started getting complicated. We wanted to know what oils were being used in the food, if there was flour in any of the sauces, and why everything had high-fructose corn syrup in it. We started making weekly trips to the grocery store so we could be sure there was real food to eat in our house. We started cooking all of our meals at home, and making enough food to take for breakfast and lunch the next day. Mary had a much longer commute home from her office than I did, so most nights, I would be the one to start cooking dinner. Before long, cooking dinner became something I looked forward to all day and I saw it as a fun way to challenge myself by coming up with different meals every night. The exciting part was trying to figure out ways to take our old favorite comfort foods and make healthier versions using the knowledge I had gained along the way. I was on websites and blogs, Pinterest and Instagram, looking at what other people were doing, and using that as inspiration for my own cooking. Don't get me wrong, it's not as if I just started whipping up masterpieces from the beginning. There was a ton of trial and error...mostly error. The more I tested, failed, and re-tested, the closer I came to mastering my recipes.

I was like a mad-scientist with my recipes. I would walk down the aisles of the grocery store, imagining all of the possibilities that could come from the ingredients I saw. I would set time aside on the weekends to test out different ideas I came up with during the week. I liked to surprise Mary each night with what I was making, only to see her face light up when she took her first bite of a healthy version of a classic dish.

(Continued...)

It became even more fun as I discovered new companies with products and ingredients that complimented my cooking. I started documenting the meals I cooked on my social media accounts every so often and would always begin the post with, "Dinner for Mary." People loved it. Friends and family started asking what I was making for dinner that night, and were drooling over the pictures of the food. After a while, I decided to start an Instagram account that solely focused on the food I was making every night. I called it "dinnerformary," in hopes of inspiring other people (and other guys) to cook delicious, healthy, real food, like I do.

There are so many kitchen gadgets on the market these days. Which ones are going help you in creating masterful meals, and which ones are just going to take up space, sitting on the counter?

Here's a list of my favorite culinary gear that will help take your cooking to the next level!

1. **Airfryer** – You will see this beautiful piece of machinery pop up in many of my recipes. I love my Airfryer so much, that I bought two! The Airfryer works by combining heat with a powerful dual fan convection system to circulate hot air around food for fast, crispy results. This type of heating and cooking requires little to no oil, making for healthier meals that taste just like old favorites. My Airfryer of choice is the Black & Decker "Purifry," but there are many good brands available. You can easily find them online at Amazon.
www.amazon.com

2. **Sous Vide Precision Cooker** – Cooking Sous Vide use to be reserved for restaurants and professional chefs, but now there are many consumer-brand precision cookers available at very reasonable prices. Sous Vide is a French style of cooking that uses the steady temperature of a water bath to cook food that is vacuum sealed in an airtight bag or container. This technique makes cooking meats and fish fool-proof. The precision cooker maintains the same temperature throughout the cooking process so your submerged food never gets over-cooked, or under-cooked. The precision cooker I like is the Anova Culinary Precision Cooker with Bluetooth and WiFi. This was a game-changer for me. With the WiFi ability, I can set up my meals in the morning before I go to work, and start the precision cooker from my phone later in the day. Then, when I get home from the office or the gym, the food is cooked and ready!
www.anovaculinary.com

3. **Baking Steel** – I heard about this bad boy when I was researching my pizza recipe. I had seen pizza stones and pizza pans that go in the oven to help cook the pizza, but this is a 15 lb piece of steel that sits on the top rack of the oven that conducts and evenly distributes heat like nothing else.
www.bakingsteel.com

4. **Spiral Slicer** – A must-have for creating everyone's favorite spaghetti alternative: Zoodles! This spiral slicer comes with four different blades and can make noodles and ribbons from many different fruits and vegetables. My favorite model is the Paderno World Cuisine Vegetable Spiral Slicer.
www.padernousa.com

(Continued...)

3

5. Meat Thermometer – An instant-read meat thermometer will be your best friend. It takes the guess-work out of figuring out when your meat is ready to serve. This little helper comes in very handy when using the Airfryer. You'll have all of your meat temperatures memorized before you know it and will be a meat expert in no time! The absolute best instant-read meat thermometer on the market is the ThermoWorks Thermapen.
www.thermoworks.com

6. Tortilla Press – You're definitely going to want a solid tortilla press when making my grain-free tortillas. It will speed up your time in the kitchen and give you professional-looking tortillas. You're going to want a durable cast-iron press to get the perfect thickness of tortilla. I like the 8" IMUSA 85008 Press that is available on Amazon.
www.amazon.com

7. Vitamix – It may look like a regular blender, but this impressive machine can do it all. With extremely powerful blades capable of pulverizing even the toughest ingredients, the Vitamix acts not only as an impressive blender, but also as a dynamic food processor. It is an expensive piece of equipment, but definitely one you will be glad you made the investment in for years to come.
www.vitamix.com

8. Vacuum Sealer – Whether it's preserving meat in the freezer or preparing a large roast for the Sous Vide Precision Cooker, a vacuum sealer is such a great tool to have. You can sleep well at night knowing with 100% certainty that no air is creeping into your sealed meals! I like the FoodSaver Vacuum Sealing System.
www.foodsaver.com

9. Crock Pot – This should be a staple in every kitchen. The crock pot was the first "set it and forget it" solution to meals. I love mine for big batches of chili and of course, for making bone broth. You can't go wrong with most brands, but I got a really great deal on a large crock pot at Costco.
www.costco.com

It took me years to discover the secret ingredients that make my recipes work so well. When we first started eating clean, there were very few companies making products that I could use in my cooking. As I experimented regularly, certain products started to shine and become staples in our meals.

THE ESSENTIALS

These products are **MUST HAVES** and will change your life just as they have changed ours.

1. Chebe Flour – I stumbled across this flour when researching how Brazilians make bread rolls from tapioca. This flour is the **BACKBONE** of my grain-free baking, and will revolutionize how you make grain-free breads. They sell the mixes in stores, but I like to buy the no-frills bread mix in bulk from their website to make sure I always have enough on hand.
www.chebe.com

2. Tapioca Flour – I discovered that using Chebe flour alone made the recipes too spongy, so pairing it with plain tapioca flour gave the recipes the perfect texture. I keep two large tubs in my pantry at all times of these two flours. One has a big "C" drawn on it, and the other has a big "T." You can find tapioca flour in stores, but I prefer to buy it in bulk online, as well.
www.nuts.com

3. Cassava Flour – Similar to Chebe and tapioca flour, cassava comes from a similar place, but has a distinct characteristic in how it bakes that makes it very special. Cassava flour is so important in my tortilla and bagel recipe, that you won't want to go without it.
www.ottosnaturals.com

4. Tiger Nut Flour – Flour made from Tiger nuts, which are actually small root vegetables that are packed with prebiotic fiber! A great one-to-one substitute for all-purpose flours.
www.nuts.com

5. OMGhee Butter – Ghee is the purified essence of butter and is often referred to as a superfood. It's loaded with omega 3 and omega 9 essential fatty acids, and is a great source of vitamins A, D, E, and K. We've tried many brands, but the creamiest, and best tasting by far is OMGhee.
www.omghee.com

6. Pork Dust – The ultimate grain-free replacement for bread crumbs. Pork Dust is finely ground pork rinds. Combined with the Airfryer, Pork Dust coated food creates healthier versions of deep-fried favorites.
www.amazon.com

(Continued...)

7. Daiya Foods Shreds – The most amazing dairy-free vegan cheese replacement. It melts just like cheese does, and is perfect in my pizza and quesadilla recipes. Found in most grocery stores.
www.daiyafoods.com

8. Kite Hill Ricotta – An unbelievable dairy-free replacement for ricotta cheese using almond milk! An absolute must for my lasagna recipe. Found in most healthy grocery stores.
www.kite-hill.com

9. Cappellos – This company has revolutionized grain-free pastas. They make gnocchi, fettuccine, and lasagna sheets without using any grain! They also have delicious grain-free chocolate chip cookie dough. You won't believe your taste buds! Found in select grocery stores in the frozen food section or online.
www.cappellos.com

10. Primal Kitchen Mayo – The healthiest mayo ever made by using avocado oil. We are obsessed with both the regular and the chipotle flavors. Never go without it! Found in most grocery stores and online.
www.primalkitchen.com

11. Frank's Red Hot – Our favorite hot sauce. Yes we put it on everything, especially wings. Found in pretty much every grocery store.
www.franksredhot.com

12. Garlic Coconut Aminos – The replacement for soy sauce! Coconut aminos are made from the sap of the coconut tree and the garlic infused version is amazing. Found in most healthy grocery stores.
www.coconutsecret.com

13. Coconut Crystals – An amazing substitute for sugar! Coconut crystals are made from the sap of coconut blossoms. This is an ideal sweetener because it is low glycemic, unrefined, and is an abundant source of minerals, 17 amino acids, vitamin C, and broad-spectrum B vitamins. Found in most healthy grocery stores.
www.coconutsecret.com

14. Raw Honey – The most important thing about honey is to make sure that it is raw. Forget those bottles of honey that are shaped like bears and pour effortlessly. You want thick, raw honey that's almost a solid. Heating up the honey kills all of the vitamins and minerals, so stay away from those squeezable honeys. My personal favorite honey is White Gold Clover Honey from Canada. Found in most healthy grocery stores.
www.whitegoldhoney.com

15. Coconut Manna – Also known as coconut butter, is made from the flesh of the coconut. When warmed up, it becomes frosting-like, and is a perfect glazing ingredient for desserts. Found in most healthy grocery stores.
www.artisanaorganics.com

THE RECIPES

You now know the Journey. You've collected the Tools, and have obtained the Essentials. You're finally ready to dive in and start creating amazingly delicious, healthy meals, just like I do.

I went through all of my recipes and hand-picked what I consider to be my Top 40, just for you. These recipes are sure to make you a hit at home or at your next dinner party. They will also give you an understanding of how my meals are created, and you will be able to branch off and start coming up with your own recipes in no time.

Good luck, and Bon Appétit!

STOVETOP BREAD STICKS (Makes 8 Bread Sticks)

Grain Free *Soy Free* *Dairy Free* *Corn Free*

WHAT YOU'LL NEED:

Large, deep pan with a lid.

1 ¼ cups - Chebe Flour

½ cup - Tapioca Flour

¼ tsp - Baking Soda

½ tsp - Cream of Tartar

2 tbsp - Olive Oil

2 - Eggs

¼ cup - Hot Water

DIRECTIONS:

Pre-heat large pan on the stovetop on **MEDIUM** heat.

1. Combine the flours, baking soda, and cream of tartar in a large bowl.

2. Add the olive oil and eggs (unbeaten) and continue to combine well.

3. Add the hot water and fold into the mix until a dough starts to form.

4. Knead the mixture until it forms a smooth dough. If dough is too sticky, sprinkle in small amounts of tapioca flour until it doesn't stick anymore.

5. Tear the dough into eight equal balls and roll between your hands to form sticks (about 4"-5" long.)

6. Place the sticks in the pan, making sure none of the sticks are touching, and cover the pan on **MEDIUM** heat for 10 minutes.

7. After 10 minutes, roll each bread stick over to cook the top-sides. Cover again for 4 minutes.

8. Remove the bread sticks from the pan and serve with OMGhee (page 5) and salt.

9

 **TORTILLAS** (Makes 6-8 Tortillas)

Grain Free *Soy Free* *Dairy Free* *Corn Free*

WHAT YOU'LL NEED:

Tortilla Press	Parchment Paper	¾ cup - Tapioca Flour	¼ cup - Olive Oil
Frying Pan	¾ Cup Cassava Flour	½ tsp - Salt	2/3 cup - Hot Water

DIRECTIONS:

Pre-heat frying pan on the stovetop on **HIGH** heat.

1. Combine the flours and salt in a large bowl. Add the olive oil and hot water to the bowl and start to fold the mixture until it becomes a smooth dough. (Use your hands towards the end.) Once the dough is formed, cover the bowl with plastic wrap to keep it warm and moist.

2. Cut parchment paper into squares that are large enough to cover the tortilla press. Open up the press and place one of these parchment paper squares on the bottom. Grab a handful of dough and lightly roll it into a ball shape. (Remember to seal the bowl back up with the plastic wrap.)

3. Place the dough ball in the center of the parchment square in the tortilla press and use your hand to flatten slightly. Take another parchment square and cover the top of the dough with it, so there is flattened dough between two pieces of parchment paper in the press. Close the press and use the handle to flatten the dough into a beautiful thin tortilla.

4. Open the press and remove the top parchment square. Take the bottom parchment square with the dough stuck to it, and place it dough-side-down in the hot pan.

5. Let it sit in the pan for about 30 seconds, until you're able to peel the parchment square off from the dough.

6. Once bubbles start to form on the top of the tortilla, flip it over for another couple of minutes. Remove tortilla from the pan and let it cool on a wire rack. Repeat until all the dough is finished.

*Tip – Make a bunch of parchment squares so you can be pressing many tortillas while one cooks at a time. Also, re-use the parchment squares as much as you can to conserve.

TORTILLAS

AMAZING SAUTEED BROCCOLI SLAW

WHAT YOU'LL NEED:

Sautée Pan w/ Lid

12 oz. Bag of Broccoli Slaw (Trader Joe's)

½ - Yellow Onion (Diced)

½ - Bell Pepper (Diced)

2 tbsp - Olive Oil

½ tbsp - Garlic Powder

½ tbsp - Onion Powder

½ tbsp - Smoked Paprika

1 tsp - Pepper

1 ½ tsp - Salt

DIRECTIONS:

1. Heat the olive oil in the pan on **MEDIUM** heat.

2. Add the diced onion and peppers.

3. When the onion starts becoming translucent, add the broccoli slaw and cover.

4. Keep the veggies covered for about 10-15 minutes, stirring occasionally every 3-4 minutes.

5. Add the salt, pepper, garlic powder, onion powder, and smoked paprika. Mix well.

6. Cover again for another 5 minutes.

7. Once the slaw is soft and bendable, it's ready to serve!

AMAZING SAUTEED BROCCOLI SLAW

13

CAULIFLOWER SPANISH RICE

Grain Free   Soy Free   Dairy Free   Corn Free

WHAT YOU'LL NEED:

Large Sautée Pan w/ Lid	1 tbsp - Onion Powder
1 - Yellow Onion (Diced)	1 tbsp - Garlic Powder
1 - Bell Pepper (Diced)	1 tbsp - Smoked Paprika
5 - Garlic Cloves (Minced)	1 tbsp - Tumeric
2 tbsp - Olive Oil	2 tsp - Pepper
1 - 8.5 oz. Jar of Sun Dried Tomatoes (In Olive Oil)	3 tsp - Salt
2 - Bags Frozen Riced Cauliflower (Trader Joe's)	
2 tbsp - Fresh Chopped Parsley	

DIRECTIONS:

1. Heat the olive oil in the pan on **MEDIUM** heat.

2. Add the minced garlic, diced onion, and diced peppers, stirring occasionally.

3. When the onion starts becoming translucent, stir in the jar of sun dried tomatoes.

4. Cover the veggie mix and let cook for 2-3 minutes.

5. Mix in the two bags of riced cauliflower and cover for 5 minutes.

6. Stir in the salt, pepper, garlic powder, onion powder, smoked paprika, and tumeric until the mix takes on a reddish/orange hue. Cover and cook for another 5 minutes.

7. Mix in the chopped parsley and cover for another 5 minutes.

8. When cauliflower is soft and spongy, it's ready to serve.

CAULIFLOWER SPANISH RICE

15

OIL-POACHED SALMON W/ GARLIC-TOMATO RED WINE AIOLI

WHAT YOU'LL NEED:

Sous Vide Precision Cooker set at 125°F

Blender

Large Bowl

Salmon Fillets

2 cups - Olive Oil

1/3 cup - Red Wine Vinegar

2 cups - Cherry Tomatoes

7 - Garlic Cloves

¼ cup - Salt

Pre-made Cauliflower Spanish Rice (page 14)

Parsley Flakes and fresh Watercress for garnish

DIRECTIONS:

1. Mix ¼ cup of salt in large bowl of cold water. Once the salt has dissolved, add your Salmon Fillets to the salt water and refrigerate for 1 hour. (This is called brining the fish. This helps properly salt the fish as well as limit that white jelly protein that comes out of salmon when it's cooked.)

2. While the salmon is brining, heat 2 cups of extra virgin olive oil on **LOW** heat in a pan. Crush the 7 cloves of garlic with the side of a knife or blunt object and add them to the olive oil, stirring occasionally.

3. After about 20 minutes of **LOW** heat, let the pan cool down on an unused burner. Once the fish is done brining, remove the fillets from the brine water and pat them dry. Place each fillet into its own quart-sized freezer Ziplock bag and add 2 Tbsp of the garlic infused olive oil from the pan. (Only add the oil, but save the garlic pieces.)

4. Using the water displacement method, seal the Ziplock bags and place them in the Sous Vide water bath set at 125°F for 20-30 minutes.

5. Once the salmon is finished in the Sous Vide bath, remove the fish from the bags and scrape off any white protein gel that may have formed. Empty the poached oil from the bags along with the remaining garlic and olive oil from the pan into your blender. Add the red wine vinegar and the cherry tomatoes to the blender and blend on high until it forms a smooth sauce. Add salt and pepper to taste.

6. If your salmon has the skin on it, you can crisp the skin a bit by either placing it skin-side-down in a hot pan, or skin-side-up in the Airfryer for two minutes at 400 degrees. To serve, scoop a hearty serving of the pre-made Cauliflower Spanish Rice and place the finished salmon fillet on top. Drizzle the garlic-tomato red wine aioli over the fish and rice and garnish with parsley flakes and/or a few sprigs of fresh watercress.

OIL-POACHED SALMON W/ GARLIC-TOMATO RED WINE AIOLI

AIRFRIED CHICKEN FINGERS W/ HONEY MUSTARD SAUCE

Grain Free Soy Free Dairy Free Corn Free

WHAT YOU'LL NEED:

Airfryer heated to 400°F

6-10 Chicken Tenders

1 - Egg (beaten)

1 bag - Pork Dust

Brown Mustard

Raw Honey

Wax Paper

Meat Thermometer

DIRECTIONS:

1. Using a 1:1 ratio, mix some raw honey and brown mustard in a bowl and set aside. (I suggest starting off with 2 tbsp of each and then adjust as needed.)

2. Pat the chicken tenders dry.

3. Pour the beaten egg into a shallow dish for the egg wash.

4. Dip one tender into the egg wash until all sides have been coated in egg.

5. In a separate bowl, completely cover the egg-washed tender with pork dust until the whole tender has been coated.

6. Place pork dust-coated tender on a large piece of wax paper and continue this process until all the tenders have been covered in pork dust.

7. Once all the tenders are dusted, gently place them in the Airfryer basket. (Keep in mind that you may need to do this in shifts as all of the tenders won't fit in the basket without piling them on top of one another. You want to make sure not to have tenders covering each other in the basket.)

8. Let the tenders cook in the Airfryer for 10-12 minutes (depending on the size of the tenders.)

9. Once the tenders reach an internal temperature of 160°F, they are ready to serve. Repeat for remaining dusted tenders, and enjoy with honey mustard dipping sauce.

*Optional Tip: Run the Pork Dust through a food processor or Vitamix on low to achieve finer dusting.

AIRFRIED CHICKEN FINGERS W/ HONEY MUSTARD SAUCE

AIRFRIED FISH STICKS

Grain Free | Soy Free | Dairy Free | Corn Free

WHAT YOU'LL NEED:

Airfryer heated to 400°F

3-5 Cod Fillets

1 - Egg (beaten)

1 bag - Pork Dust

Wax Paper

Meat Thermometer

DIRECTIONS:

1. Pat the cod fillets dry and cut them into sticks about one inch wide and four inches long.

2. Pour the beaten egg into a shallow dish for the egg wash.

3. Dip one cod stick into the egg wash until all sides have been coated in egg.

4. In a separate bowl, completely cover the egg-washed stick with pork dust until the whole stick has been coated.

5. Place pork dust-coated stick on a large piece of wax paper and continue this process until all the sticks have been covered in pork dust.

6. Once all the sticks are dusted, gently place them in the Airfryer basket. (Keep in mind that you may need to do this in shifts as all of the sticks won't fit in the basket without piling them on top of one another. It's ok to have some overlapping, but try not to cover them completely)

7. Let the sticks cook in the Airfryer for 5-10 minutes, checking their internal temperature with the meat thermometer and shaking the basket occasionally.

8. Once the sticks reach an internal temperature of 130°F, they are ready to serve. Repeat for remaining dusted sticks, and enjoy with Primal Kitchen Chiptole Mayo. (page 6)

*Optional Tip: Run the Pork Dust through a food processor or Vitamix on low to achieve finer dusting.

AIRFRIED FISH STICKS

Grain Free   Soy Free   Dairy Free   Corn Free

WHAT YOU'LL NEED:

Aifryer heated to 400°F

1 lb - Lump Crab Meat

½ cup - Primal Kitchen Mayo

1 cup - Pork Dust

1 tbsp - Dijon Mustard

1 tsp - Franks Hot Sauce

1 - Egg

2 tbsp - Fresh Chopped Parsley

½ cup - Bell Pepper (minced)

1 tbsp - Tiger Nut Flour

¼ tsp - Pepper

1 tsp - Old Bay Seasoning

Wax Paper

DIRECTIONS:

1. In a large bowl, combine the mayo, mustard, tiger nut flour, old bay, and hot sauce.

2. Add the bell pepper, egg and ground pepper.

3. Gently fold in the crab.

4. Add the pork dust and parsley, and gently mix together.

5. Once well-combined, scoop ¼ cup at a time of the mixture onto a wax paper-lined cookie sheet or cutting board and mold into a puck-shapes.

6. Once all of the mixture has been molded into pucks on the tray, put the tray in the freezer for 15 minutes.

7. After 15 minutes, transfer a few pucks at time to the Airfryer and cook at 400°F for 12-15 minutes. Once the crab cakes are perfectly browned in the Airfryer, remove and serve with Primal Kitchen Chipotle Mayo (page 6) and lemon wedges.

AIRFRIED CRAB CAKES

AIRFRIED BUTTERFLIED SHRIMP

Grain Free *Soy Free* *Dairy Free* *Corn Free*

WHAT YOU'LL NEED:

Airfryer heated to 400°F

Uncooked Jumbo Shrimp (peeled w/ tail-on)

1 - Egg (beaten)

1 bag - Pork Dust

1 tbsp - Garlic Powder

1 tbsp - Paprika

Wax Paper

DIRECTIONS:

1. Pat the shrimp dry and butterfly them by cutting a slit down the back and spreading it open. (Make sure not to cut all the way through the shrimp)

2. Pour the beaten egg into a shallow dish for the egg wash.

3. Dip one shrimp into the egg wash until all sides and edges have been coated in egg.

4. In a separate bowl, combine the pork dust, paprika, and garlic powder. Completely dust the egg-washed shrimp with the pork-dusted seasonings until the whole shrimp has been coated.

5. Place pork dust-coated shrimp on a large piece of wax paper and continue this process until all the shrimp have been covered in pork dust.

6. Once all the shrimp are dusted, gently place them in the Airfryer basket. (Keep in mind that you may need to do this in shifts as all of the shrimp won't fit in the basket without piling them on top of one another. Try not to have any shrimp overlapping in the basket.)

7. Let the shrimp cook in the Airfryer for 10 minutes for each batch.

8. Repeat for remaining dusted shrimp, and enjoy with Primal Kitchen Chiptole Mayo (page 6)

*Optional Tip: Run the Pork Dust through a food processor or Vitamix on low to achieve finer dusting.

AIRFRIED BUTTERFLIED SHRIMP

AIRFRIED SCOTCH EGG

Grain Free   Soy Free   Dairy Free   Corn Free

WHAT YOU'LL NEED:

Airfryer heated to 400°F

Large Pot

5 - Large Eggs

1 bag - Pork Dust

1 lb - Italian Sausage

DIRECTIONS:

1. First, we need to **MEDIUM** boil four of the eggs. You can accomplish this by placing the four eggs in a pot and filling it with cold water 1" above the tops of the eggs.

2. Heat the pot on the stove on **HIGH** heat until the water boils.

3. Once the water boils, remove the pot from the stove and let it sit for 4 minutes.

4. After 4 minutes, gently remove the eggs with a slotted spoon from the hot water, and place them in an ice bath for 30 minutes.

5. Remove the eggs from the ice bath and gently peel away all of the shells.

6. Separate the Italian sausage into four equal parts and wrap the outside of each egg in sausage, covering the whole egg.

7. Beat the uncooked egg, making an egg wash.

8. Brush the sausage-covered eggs with the egg wash until they are well coated with egg.

9. Thoroughly cover the egg-washed sausage with pork dust so that no sausage is visible.

10. Place dusted eggs into the Airfryer set at 400°F for 15 minutes. Remove from the Airfryer and serve on top of salad or my Amazing Sautéed Broccoli Slaw (page 12) and hot sauce!

AIRFRIED SCOTCH EGG

27

BAGELS (Makes 8 medium bagels or 4 large bagels)

Grain Free Soy Free Dairy Free Corn Free

WHAT YOU'LL NEED: *Optional – Sesame Seeds / Poppy Seeds / 2 tbsp ground cinnamon / Raisins

Large pot	2 cups - Chebe Flour	1 tsp - Baking Soda	¾ cup - Warm Water
Large Bowl	½ cup - Tapioca Flour	2 tsp - Cream of Tartar	Parchment Paper
4 - Eggs	1 cup - Cassava Flour	¼ cup - Olive Oil	

DIRECTIONS:

1. Preheat your oven to 500°F. Fill the large pot with water (about ¾ full) and heat it on the stovetop on HIGH heat to bring it to a boil.

2. In a large bowl, combine the flours, baking soda, and cream of tartar. (If making Cinnamon Raisin Bagels, add the cinnamon now too.)

3. Add the eggs and olive oil and mix well. (If making Cinnamon Raisin Bagels, add the raisins now too.)

4. Once the mixture forms into a dry dough, add the warm water and fold and knead until a soft dough forms. (If the dough is too sticky, add small amounts of tapioca flour until it becomes more workable, but be careful not to dry it out too much.) Separate the dough into either 8 medium balls, or 4 large balls.

5. Using your finger, poke a hole through the center of each ball and form them into bagel-shapes. (The center hole should be about 1" in diameter for the medium bagels and 2" in diameter for the large bagels.)

6. Once the pot of water reaches a boil, gently drop the bagels into the boiling water for 2 minutes. After 2 minutes, rotate the bagels so that the side facing down is now facing up for another 2 minutes. After the 4 minutes in the boiling water is up, gently remove the bagels from the water and place the bagels on a large piece of parchment paper. (The bagels will have "puffed up" considerably in the water.)

7. If you are making poppy or sesame bagels, sprinkle your bagels with either poppy seeds or sesame seeds on the parchment paper, to your liking.

8. Place the bagels in the 500°F preheated oven for 10 minutes. (You can either transfer them directly onto the Baking Steel (page 3) if you have one, or simply transfer the bagels on the parchment paper to a cookie sheet.)

9. After 10 minutes, turn the oven OFF and let the bagels rest in the oven for another 10 minutes. Remove the bagels and enjoy!

BAGELS

Grain Free   *Soy Free*   *Dairy Free*   *Corn Free*

WHAT YOU'LL NEED: *Optional Protein – Chopped Cooked Chicken / Steak / Shrimp

Airfryer heated to 400°F	1 - Medium Yellow Onion (chopped)
Tortillas (page 10)	1 cup - Mushrooms (chopped)
1 bag - Daiya Foods Dairy-Free Shreds	1 - Bell Pepper (diced)
1 tbsp - Olive Oil	

DIRECTIONS:

1. Heat the olive oil in a pan on **MEDIUM** heat and add the onion and mushrooms.

2. Once the onion becomes translucent and the mushrooms soften, remove the pan from the heat and let it cool.

3. Chop the Daiya Shreds into small pieces.

4. Take a tortilla and sprinkle the chopped Daiya shreds on top, covering it well.

5. Layer some of the sauteed onions and mushrooms, diced bell peppers, and cooked protein next.

6. Add some more chopped Daiya shreds on top and cover with another tortilla.

7. Heat the tortilla in the microwave on **HIGH** for 1 min.

8. After 1 minute in the microwave, transfer the tortilla to the 400°F heated **Airfryer** and cook for 3 minutes.

9. Remove from the Airfryer and cut into four pieces using a pizza cutter. Enjoy with guacamole, or some Primal Kitchen Chipotle Mayo (Page 6)

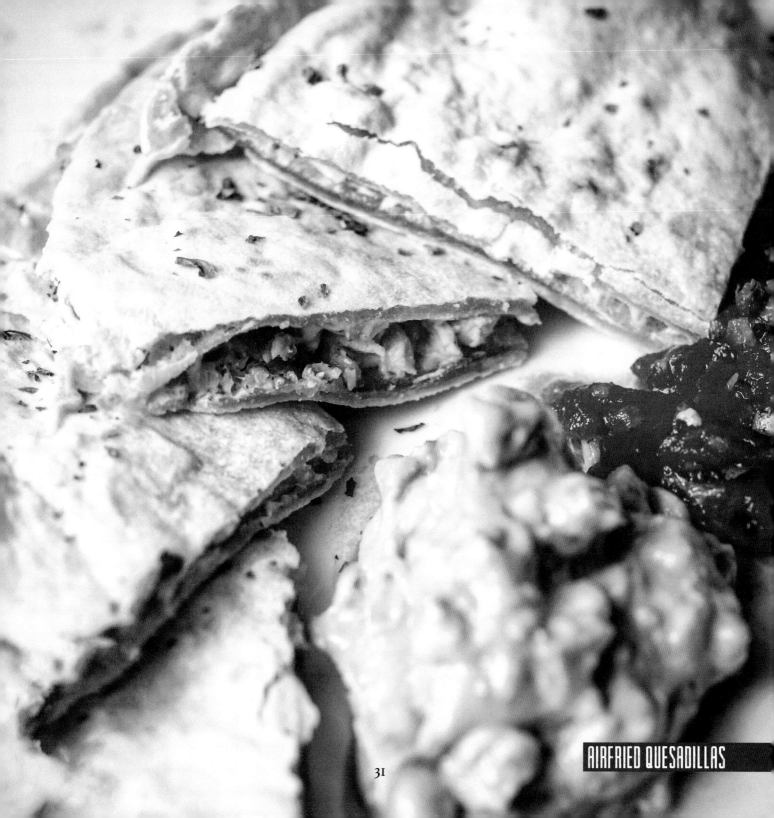

AIRFRIED QUESADILLAS

SESAME TUNA W/ GARLIC COCONUT AMINOS

Grain Free   Soy Free   Dairy Free   Corn Free

WHAT YOU'LL NEED:

Cauliflower Spanish Rice (page 14)

Cast Iron Skillet

Tuna Steaks

1 tbsp - Avocado Oil

Garlic Coconut Aminos

Sesame Seeds

DIRECTIONS:

1. Heat the avocado oil in a cast iron skillet over **HIGH** heat until oil starts to smoke.

2. Coat the tuna steaks in garlic coconut aminos and cover with sesame seeds.

3. Place the tuna steaks in the pan, and sear for about 30 seconds on each side.

4. Serve on top of Cauliflower Spanish Rice (Page 14) with more coconut aminos.

SESAME TUNA W/ GARLIC COCONUT AMINOS

33

COCONUT YELLOW CURRY W/ SHRIMP

WHAT YOU'LL NEED:

Large Pot

5 tbsp - Thai Yellow Curry Paste

2 tbsp - Olive Oil

1 - Large Sweet Potato (peeled and cubed)

2 cups - Broccoli Florets

2 - Large Carrots (chopped)

1 - Large Yellow Onion (cut in strips)

1 - Red Bell Pepper (chopped)

2 cups - Sliced Mushrooms

1 bunch - Watercress

1 lb - Raw Shrimp (peeled)

2 Cans - Coconut Milk

1 Can - Coconut Cream

DIRECTIONS:

1. Heat the olive oil in the large pot on **MEDIUM** heat and stir in the curry paste.

2. Add one can of coconut milk to the pot, followed by the cubed sweet potato and cover for 5 minutes.

3. Stir in the broccoli, carrots, and shrimp followed by the other can of coconut milk and cover.

4. When the shrimp is red and cooked, stir in the mushrooms, peppers, and onions and cover for another 5 minutes.

5. Reduce the heat to **LOW** and stir in the can of coconut cream. When the sweet potato and broccoli is cooked through and soft, serve in a bowl with a garnish of fresh watercress.

COCONUT YELLOW CURRY W/ SHRIMP

AIRFRIED HOT WINGS

WHAT YOU'LL NEED:

Airfryer heated to 400°F

Large Bowl

8-12 Chicken Wings

2 tbsp - Olive Oil

1½ tsp - Salt

1 tsp - Pepper

Frank's Hot Sauce

DIRECTIONS:

1. In the large bowl, toss the chicken wings with the salt, pepper, and olive oil so that all the wings are well coated.

2. Place the wings in the Airfryer basket, and cook at 400°F for 20-25 minutes, making sure to toss them every 5 minutes or so to make sure all pieces get cooked.

3. Once all of the wings get golden-brown, remove them from the Airfryer and place them back in the large bowl (make sure you've cleaned the bowl since the raw chicken was in it) tossing them now with Franks Hot Sauce (use as much as you need to cover the wings.)

4. Place the wings back in the Airfryer and let them cook for another 5 minutes with the hot sauce coating. After they are finished, serve the wings with a fresh drizzle of hot sauce on top.

37

AIRFRIED HOT WINGS

AIRFRIED CHICKEN THIGHS

Grain Free

Soy Free

Corn Free

WHAT YOU'LL NEED:

Airfryer heated to 400°F

Chicken Thighs (skin-on)

OMGhee Butter

Salt

Pepper

Garlic Powder

Onion Powder

Rosemary

DIRECTIONS:

1. Coat the chicken thighs in OMGhee completely.

2. Season the thighs by sprinkling a pinch of the following on top of each: salt, pepper, garlic powder, onion powder, and rosemary.

3. Place the thighs skin-side-up in the Airfryer and cook at 400°F for 10-15 min.

4. Use your meat thermometer to check the internal temperature of the thighs. Once the thighs reach an internal temperature of 160°F, remove and serve with a side of veggies or on top of my Amazing Sautéed Broccoli Slaw. (page 12)

AIRFRIED CHICKEN THIGHS

AIRFRIED HONEY·CURRY CHICKEN DRUMETTES

Grain Free Soy Free Dairy Free Corn Free

WHAT YOU'LL NEED:

Airfryer heated to 400°F

Large Bowl

8-12 Chicken Wing Drumettes

2 tbsp - Olive Oil

1½ tsp - Salt

1 tsp - Pepper

¼ cup - Raw Honey

2 tbsp - Curry Powder

DIRECTIONS:

1. In the large bowl, toss the chicken drumettes with the salt, pepper, and olive oil so that all the drumettes are well coated.

2. Place the drumettes in the Airfryer basket, and cook at 400°F for 20-25 minutes, making sure to toss them every 5 minutes or so to make sure all pieces get cooked.

3. While drumettes are being cooked, mix the raw honey with the curry powder to form a paste.

4. Once all of the drumettes are golden-brown, remove them from the Airfryer and place them back in the large bowl (make sure you've cleaned the bowl since the raw chicken was in it) tossing them now with the honey-curry paste (use as much as you need to cover the drumettes).

5. Place the drumettes back in the Airfryer and let them cook for another 5 minutes with the honey-curry coating. After they are finished, serve the drumettes with a fresh drizzle of any remaining honey-curry paste.

AIRFRIED HONEY·CURRY CHICKEN DRUMETTES

41

 **PASTA MAMA**

Grain Free | Soy Free | Dairy Free | Corn Free

WHAT YOU'LL NEED:

1 package - Cappellos Grain-Free Fettuccine

8-10 oz. - Cooked Chicken Breast (chopped)

1 - Large Egg (beaten)

2 tbsp - Olive Oil

¼ tsp - Salt

¼ tsp - Garlic Powder

¼ tsp - Dried Oregano

¼ tsp - Onion Powder

2 - Garlic Cloves (minced)

2 tbsp - Parsley (chopped)

DIRECTIONS:

1. Boil water in a large pot. While the water is boiling, heat the olive oil in a large pan on **MEDIUM-LOW** heat

2. Once the oil starts to shimmer, add in the minced garlic, salt, oregano, onion powder, and garlic powder. Let it cook for about 2 minutes, stirring occasionally.

3. Add in the chopped parsley. Once the parsley has been added, it's time to cook the pasta. Place the fettuccine in the boiling water for exactly **90 SECONDS**.

4. After 90 seconds in the boiling water, remove the fettuccine by pouring into a colander or strainer and then quickly rinse with **COLD** water.

5. Add the fettuccine to the pan and add 1 tbsp of **HOT** water. Stir everything for about 1-2 minutes.

6. Stir in the cooked chicken pieces, and then pour the beaten egg over everything in the pan. Make sure to keep mixing and folding as soon as you pour in the egg so that all of the ingredients are well-coated with the egg. Do this for about 2-3 minutes and then serve!

PASTA MAMA

PIZZA

Grain Free   *Soy Free*   *Dairy Free*   *Corn Free*

WHAT YOU'LL NEED: *Optional Toppings – Bell Peppers, Onions, Mushrooms, Pepperoni...etc

Parchment Paper	1 tbsp - Garlic Powder
Dough from Stovetop Bread Sticks (page 8)	1 tbsp - Dried Oregano
1 - 6 oz. Can of Tomato Paste	1 tbsp - Onion Powder
1 bag - Daiya Foods Mozzarella Shreds	1 tbsp - Dried Basil
1 ½ tsp - Salt	1 tsp - Pepper

DIRECTIONS:

1. Pre-Heat oven to 500°F. Make the dough from my bread sticks recipe. (page 8)

2. Once the dough is made, place it on a large piece of parchment paper and use the palm of your hand to press it into a large circle. (Try to keep a thicker rim around the edge of the circle to make a fluffier crust.)

3. In a bowl, empty the can of tomato paste and then use the empty can to add a can-full of water. Mix together until it forms a sauce, adding the salt, pepper, oregano, basil, onion and garlic powders.

4. Spread the sauce evenly over the dough and add whatever toppings you like. Finish by covering the pizza with Daiya Mozzarella Shreds.

5. Transfer the pizza and parchment paper onto a cookie sheet and then set it on the top rack of the 500°F oven and let it cook for 10 minutes. (You can transfer the pizza easily with a pizza peel or you can just slide it onto the cookie sheet. If you have the Baking Steel (page 3) already in your oven or a pizza stone, transfer the pizza and parchment paper directly onto it. If not, the cookie sheet will suffice.)

6. After 10 minutes, remove from the oven, slice, and enjoy!

PIZZA

LASAGNA

Grain Free   Soy Free   Dairy Free   Corn Free

WHAT YOU'LL NEED:

1 package - Cappellos Grain-Free Lasagna Sheets

1 ½ lb - Ground Beef

1 ½ lb - Ground Italian Sausage

1 - Large Onion (minced)

6-7 cloves - Garlic (Crushed)

1 - 28oz. Can Crushed Tomatoes

4 tbsp - Chopped Parsley

2 packages - Kite Hill Dairy-Free Ricotta

1 bag - Daiya Foods Mozzarella Shreds

2 - Large Eggs

2 - 6oz. Cans Tomato Paste

2 tbsp - Garlic powder

2 tbsp - Dried Oregano

2 tbsp - Onion Powder

2 tbsp - Dried Basil

½ cup - Water

2 ½ tsp - Salt

DIRECTIONS:

1. Preheat oven to 375°F

2. In a large pot, cook the ground beef, Italian sausage, onion, and crushed garlic over medium heat until well browned.

3. Stir in the crushed tomatoes, tomato paste, and ½ cup of water. Add the garlic powder, dried oregano, onion powder, basil, 2 tbsp of the chopped parsley, 1 ½ tsp salt, and the pepper.

4. In a medium bowl, combine the 2 packages of Kite Hill ricotta cheese with the 2 eggs, 2 tbsp of the chopped parsley, and 1 tsp salt until it's well mixed.

5. In a deep baking dish, spread some of the meat sauce at the bottom. Then, arrange some of the lasagna noodles over top, covering the sauce layer. Spread some of the ricotta cheese mix on top of the noodles and cover with some of the Daiya Mozzarella cheese. Spoon more meat sauce over top, and more mozzarella, then repeat the layers with the noodles etc. Finish with the lasagna noodles on top, covered with a layer of mozzarella.

6. Cover with foil, and bake for 25 minutes. Then, remove the foil and bake uncovered for another 25 minutes. Serve and enjoy!

LASAGNA

ASPARAGUS & SAUSAGE GNOCCHI

Grain Free   Soy Free   Dairy Free   Corn Free

WHAT YOU'LL NEED:

1 package - Cappellos Grain-Free Gnocchi

½ lb - Spicy Italian Sausage

1 bunch - Asparagus (chopped)

2 tbsp - Fresh Parsley (chopped)

½ tbsp - Smoked Paprika

DIRECTIONS:

1. Add the gnocchi to 3-4 quarts of boiling water and stir gently to avoid sticking. Continue to stir every 30 seconds for approximately 3-5 minutes. When the gnocchi float, they're done.

2. Remove gnocchi from the water with a slotted spoon or strainer.

3. Add the Italian Sausage and chopped asparagus to a large pan on **MEDIUM** heat. Brown the sausage, letting the fat cook the asparagus as well. Once the sausage has browned, and the asparagus is tender, stir in the gnocchi.

4. Salt and pepper to taste, and serve with fresh chopped parsley garnish and a sprinkle of smoked paprika.

ASPARAGUS & SAUSAGE GNOCCHI

49

STROMBOLI

Grain Free *Soy Free* *Dairy Free* *Corn Free*

WHAT YOU'LL NEED: *Optional Toppings – Bell Peppers, Onions, Mushrooms, Pepperoni...etc

Parchment Paper

Dough from Stovetop Bread Sticks (page 8)

1 - 6 oz. Can of Tomato Paste

1 bag - Daiya Foods Mozzarella Shreds

1 - Egg (beaten)

1 ½ tsp - Salt

1 tbsp - Garlic Powder

1 tbsp - Dried Oregano

1 tbsp - Onion Powder

1 tbsp - Dried Basil

1 tsp - Pepper

DIRECTIONS:

1. Pre-Heat the oven to 400°F. Make the dough from my bread sticks recipe. (page 8)

2. Place the dough on a large piece of parchment paper and use a rolling pin to make a big rectangle.

3. In a bowl, empty the can of tomato paste and then use the empty can to add a can-full of water. Mix together until it forms a sauce, adding the salt, pepper, oregano, basil, onion and garlic powders.

4. Spread the sauce evenly over the dough (making sure to leave about 2 inches uncovered on one of the long sides for when we roll it) and add whatever toppings you like, finishing by covering the toppings with Daiya mozzarella shreds.

5. Brush the beaten egg on the empty 2 inch edge, and fold up the short sides about an inch, brushing egg on the tops of the flaps you just made too.

6. Roll the Stromboli up as tight as you can, making sure you end up with the egg-covered 2 inch strip on the bottom at the end. Then, brush egg on top of the rolled Stromboli. With a sharp knife, cut some small slits in the top and sprinkle with parsley flakes.

7. Transfer the Stromboli and parchment paper onto a cookie sheet. Set it on the top rack of the 400°F oven and let it cook for 20 minutes. (You can transfer the stromboli easily with a pizza peel or you can just slide it onto the cookie sheet. If you have the Baking Steel (page 3) already in your oven or a pizza stone, transfer the stromboli and parchment paper directly onto it. If not, the cookie sheet will suffice.) After 20 minutes, remove, slice into segments, and enjoy!

STROMBOLI

MEATBALLS W/ ZOODLES

Grain Free   Soy Free   Dairy Free   Corn Free

WHAT YOU'LL NEED:

1 lb - Ground Beef

1 lb - Ground Veal

1 lb - Ground Italian Sausage

1 ½ tsp - Salt

6-7 - Garlice Cloves (minced)

½ - Onion (minced)

½ tsp - Pepper

1 tsp - Dried Oregano

1 tsp - Dried Basil

2 - Eggs (beaten)

1 cup - Pork Dust

½ cup - Daiya Mozzarella Shreds (minced)

2 tbsp - Fresh Parsley (chopped)

3 - Large Zucchinis (peeled)

DIRECTIONS:

1. In a large bowl, combine all meats, followed by all the other ingredients except for the zuchinni.

2. Form into large balls and place evenly on a baking sheet. Place in a 400° F oven and bake for 18-22 minutes uncovered.

3. Using your Spiral Slicer (page 3), spiralize the zuchinni to create your zoodles. Place your newly made zoodles in the Airfryer at 250° F while the meatballs bake in the oven. (Make sure you routinely check on the zoodles in the Airfryer to make sure they are not burning. The goal is to drain some of the moisture out of the zoodles.)

4. Serve the finished meatballs over the zoodles and add my tomato sauce (from my pizza recipe, page 44.)

MEATBALLS W/ ZOODLES

53

COCONUT CREAM VIRGIN VODKA SAUCE

Grain Free   Soy Free   Dairy Free   Corn Free

WHAT YOU'LL NEED:

1 can - Coconut Cream

1 - 8.5 oz. Jar Sun Dried Tomatoes (in Olive Oil)

1 can - Artichoke Hearts in Water (chopped)

1 cup - Mushrooms (sliced)

1 - Large Onion (sliced)

5 - Garlic Cloves (minced)

2 tbsp - Fresh Parsley (chopped)

1 ½ tsp - Salt

½ tsp - Pepper

1 tbsp - Olive Oil

DIRECTIONS:

1. In a large pan, heat the olive oil over **LOW** heat and add the minced garlic and onion, stirring occasionally.

2. Once the onions become translucent, add in the mushrooms and sundried tomatoes.

3. Stir in the artichoke hearts and parsley, then season with the salt and pepper.

4. Once everything in the pan has cooked together for a few minutes, add the coconut cream and let it melt into the ingredients. Stir one last time to combine everything and then serve with your favorite protein!

COCONUT CREAM VIRGIN VODKA SAUCE

AIRFRIED SWEET POTATO BOATS

Grain Free   Soy Free   Dairy Free   Corn Free

WHAT YOU'LL NEED:

Airfryer heated to 400°F

2 - Large Sweet Potatoes

½ lb - Ground Beef

½ cup - Mushrooms (sliced)

¼ cup - Onion (minced)

1 - Ripe Avocado

2 - Garlic Cloves (minced)

1 tsp - Salt

½ tsp - Pepper

1 tsp - Chili Powder

1 tbsp - Olive Oil

DIRECTIONS:

1. Using a fork, poke holes in the sweet potatoes and lightly coat the outsides in olive oil. Then, place them in the Airfryer at 400°F for 45 minutes.

2. While the sweet potatoes are cooking, in a large pan, heat the olive oil over **MEDIUM** heat and add the minced onions and garlic.

3. When the onions start becoming tanslucent, add the mushrooms and cook together for 5 minutes. Then, add the ground beef and let it brown with the mushrooms, onions, and garlic.

4. Once the beef is pretty well browned, stir in the salt, pepper, and chili powder.

5. When the sweet potatoes are finished in the Airfryer, cut them in half and scoop out the center using a spoon. (Save the center and add it on the plate.) Fill the sweet potato boats with the cooked meat from the pan and top with the avocado slices.

6. Sprinkle a pinch more salt and a dash more of chili powder on top and enjoy!

AIRFRIED SWEET POTATO BOATS

AIRFRIED STUFFED PEPPERS

Grain Free   Soy Free   Corn Free

WHAT YOU'LL NEED:

Airfryer heated to 400°F

2 - Large Bell Peppers (tops cut off & insides removed)

½ lb - Ground Italian Sausage

¼ cup - Mushrooms (diced)

¼ cup - Onion (minced)

Daiya Foods Shreds

1 tbsp - Olive Oil

OMGhee Butter

Salt

Pepper

DIRECTIONS:

1. In a large pan, heat the olive oil over **MEDIUM** heat and start browning the Italian sausage.

2. While the sausage is cooking, coat the peppers in OMGhee Butter and place them in the Airfryer at 400°F for 10 minutes.

3. When the sausage begins to brown, add the onions and mushrooms. Let the ingredients cook together for 5 minutes.

4. Fill the peppers with the cooked sausage, onions, and mushrooms and top with a handful of Daiya Foods Shreds. Place the peppers back in the Airfryer for another 5 minutes or so, until the shreds become melted.

5. Once done, carefully remove the stuffed peppers with tongs and serve!

AIRFRIED STUFFED PEPPERS

59

Grain Free   Soy Free   Dairy Free   Corn Free

WHAT YOU'LL NEED:

Cappellos Grain-Free Fettuccine

1 - Egg (beaten)

Daiya Foods Cheddar Shreds

Prosciutto (cut into small pieces)

DIRECTIONS:

1. Start to boil water in a pot. While the water is boiling, take a large knife or kitchen scissors and cut the fettuccine into 1" pieces.

2. When the water reaches a rolling boil, add the cut-up fettuccine and let them cook in the boiling water for exactly 90 seconds.

3. When the 90 seconds are up, pour the fettuccine into a strainer to drain all of the water out, and rinse under cold water for a few seconds.

4. Heat a small pot on **LOW** heat on the stovetop and add the cooked fettuccine and half the bag of cheddar shreds. Add the beaten egg and start stirring.

5. Stir continuously and at a good pace so that the egg doesn't have time to set on its own.

6. Once the cheddar shreds have melted completely and combined with the egg and fettuccine, stir in the prosciutto and serve!

MAC & CHEESE

PULLED PORK W/ SAUTEED APPLES

Grain Free   Soy Free   Dairy Free   Corn Free

WHAT YOU'LL NEED:

Crock Pot

3-5 lb pork Shoulder

6 - Granny Smith Apples
  (peeled & slied into thin wedges)

3 tbsp - Coconut Crystals

1 tbsp - Tapioca Flour

FOR THE DRY RUB:

1 tbsp of the following:
- Salt
- Smoked Paprika
- Garlic powder
- Mustard Powder
- Onion Powder
- Dried Basil
- Coconut Crystals
- Dried Rosemary

½ tbsp - Pepper

DIRECTIONS:

1. Combine the ingredients for the dry-rub in a bowl and rub on the pork, covering as much of the meat as possible.

2. Place the rubbed shoulder in the crock pot on **LOW** and let it cook for 24 hrs.

3. When the shoulder is close to being done, place the sliced apples in a large covered pan and cook on **LOW** on the stovetop.

4 When the apples start to soften, stir in the coconut crystals and let them cook for another 2-3 minutes.

5. Stir in the tapioca flour to make the apples congeal a bit.

6. Take the pork out of the crock pot, put it in a large bowl and shred it by pulling the meat apart with two large forks. Serve with the sautéed apples and enjoy!

PULLED PORK W/ SAUTEED APPLES

FENNEL PORK CHOPS

Grain Free   Soy Free   Dairy Free   Corn Free

WHAT YOU'LL NEED:

Sous Vide Precision Cooker at 140°F

Large Pan

Cast Iron Skillet

2-4 Boneless Pork Chops

2 tbsp - Olive Oil

2 - Fennel Bulbs (trimmed and thinly sliced)

1 tbsp - Lemon Juice

1 Sprig - Fresh Thyme

1 Sprig - Fresh Oregano

2 - Garlic Cloves (peeled and lightly crushed)

Chopped Fresh Parsley

Salt

Pepper

DIRECTIONS:

1. Generously season the pork chops with salt and pepper. Place in a large ziplock or vacuum seal bag and seal the bag using the water immersion technique or a vacuum sealer. Place in the water bath for 1 hour at 140°F.

2. While the chops are in the water, heat 1 tbsp of the olive oil in a large skillet over **MEDIUM/LOW** heat. Add the fennel and season with salt, stirring occasionally until softened and golden (about 45 minutes.) Stir in lemon juice and set aside to keep warm.

3. When the pork chops are finished in the bath, remove them from the bag and pat dry. Place the remaining tbsp of olive oil, thyme, oregano, and garlic in a cast iron skillet over **MEDIUM/LOW** heat. Gently cook the herbs in the oil until the garlic just begins to brown, 5 to 7 minutes. Then, remove the herbs.

4. Increase the heat under the skillet to **HIGH**. When the oil just begins to smoke, add the pork chops and sear until golden brown, about 1 minute per side.

5. Serve with pork chops on top of fennel and garnish with fennel fronds, parsley, and a drizzle of olive oil.

FENNEL PORK CHOPS

AIRFRIED MAPLE-PECAN PORK TENDERLOIN

Grain Free   Soy Free   Corn Free

WHAT YOU'LL NEED:

Airfryer set to 400°F

1-1.5 lb - Pork Tenderloin

OMGhee Butter

Maple Syrup (Grade B)

Raw Pecan Pieces

Chopped Fresh Parsley

1 tsp - Salt

1 tsp -Pepper

DIRECTIONS:

1. Pre-Heat the Airfryer to 400°F. Coat the tenderloin in OMGhee Butter and season with salt and pepper.

2. Cook the tenderloin in the Airfryer for 20 minutes.

3. Once the tenderloin reaches an internal temperature of 140°F, slice into medallions and drizzle with maple syrup. Garnish with sprinkled pecan pieces and parsley.

AIRFRIED MAPLE-PECAN PORK TENDERLOIN

67

AIRFRIED LAMB CHOPS W/ DILL SAUCE

Grain Free

Soy Free

Corn Free

WHAT YOU'LL NEED:

Airfryer set to 400°

1-1.5 lb - Lamb Chops

OMGhee Butter

¾ cup - Primal Kitchen Mayonnaise

1 tsp - Lemon Juice

½ tbsp - Dill Fronds

1 tsp - Salt

1 tsp -Pepper

DIRECTIONS:

1. Pre-Heat the Airfryer to 400°F. Coat the Lamb Chops in OMGhee Butter and season with salt and pepper.

2. Cook the chops in the Airfryer for 15-18 minutes.

3. Combine the mayonnaise, lemon juice, and dill, making a sauce.

4. Use your meat thermometer and once the chops reach an internal temperature of 140°F, serve with the dill sauce.

AIRFRIED LAMB CHOPS W/ DILL SAUCE

69

Grain Free   *Soy Free*   *Dairy Free*   *Corn Free*

WHAT YOU'LL NEED:

Crock Pot

2 - Carrots (chopped)

2 - Celery Stalks (chopped)

1 - Onion (chopped)

7 - Garlic Cloves (smashed)

2-3 lbs - Chicken Feet or Beef Bones

2 - Bay Leaves

3 tsp - Salt

Whole Peppercorns

2 tbsp - Apple Cider Vinegar

Water

DIRECTIONS:

1. Place all of the vegetables in the bottom of the crock pot.

2. Layer the chicken feet/beef bones on top. Tuck in the bay leaves between them.

3. Sprinkle the salt, add a handful of peppercorns, and drizzle the apple cider vinegar on top.

4. Fill the crock pout with water so that the ingredients are covered and set on **LOW** for 24 hours.

5. When finished, remove the large vegetables and bones with a slotted spoon and strain the rest to get the pure golden broth.

You can freeze any extra broth and enjoy later.

BONE BROTH

BACON-WRAPPED DATES

Grain Free Soy Free Dairy Free Corn Free

WHAT YOU'LL NEED:

1 carton - Medjool Dates

Pecan Pieces

1 package - Bacon (sugar & nitrate free)

Toothpicks

DIRECTIONS:

1. Pre-Heat the oven to 400°F.

2. Soak the dates in hot water for 20 minutes so the skin becomes soft.

3. Remove the skin and pits from the dates and set the date meat aside.

4. Cut the bacon strips into thirds. This will give you more bacon pieces to work with because you can stretch the smaller strips around the dates.

5. Take a skinned date and put a couple pieces of pecan in the center. Close the date and then wrap with one of the bacon pieces. (Don't be afraid to stretch it out to fit around the date.) Secure the bacon strip with a toothpick. Repeat this for all of the dates and line them up in rows on a large baking sheet.

6. Bake in the oven at 400°F for 20-25 minutes or until the bacon is cooked to your liking. Let cool, and serve!

BACON-WRAPPED DATES

BLONDIES

WHAT YOU'LL NEED:

1 ¼ cups - Chebe Flour

½ cup - Tapioca Flour

¾ cup (6 oz.) - OMGhee Butter

1 ½ cups - Coconut Crystals

2 - Eggs

1 ½ tsp - Vanilla Extract

6 oz. - 70% Dark Chocolate Baking Chunks

DIRECTIONS:

1. Preheat oven to 350°F. In a large bowl, use a hand mixer and mix the coconut crystals and the OMGhee Butter until well combined.

2. Add the eggs and vanilla extract and mix well. Add the dry flours and keep mixing until a batter forms.

3. Fold in the dark chocolate chunks and transfer mix into a 9" x 9" square baking dish. (I use the silicone ones.) Make sure to even out the batter in the dish so it fills each side evenly.

4. Bake in the oven at 350°F for 20-25 minutes or until top is browned and you can insert a toothpick in the center and remove it cleanly.

5. Let cool, divide into brownie squares, and serve.

BLONDIES

CINNAMON ROLLS (Makes 8 rolls)

Grain Free — Soy Free — Corn Free

WHAT YOU'LL NEED:

Large Oven-Safe pan w/ Lid

Parchment Paper

1 tbsp - Coconut oil

FILLING

½ cup (4 oz.) - OMGhee Butter

1 cup - Coconut Crystals

6 tbsp - Apple Sauce

2 tbsp - Tiger Nut Flour

2 tsp - Cinnamon

DOUGH

3 ½ cups - Chebe Flour

2 tbsp - Olive Oil

4 - Eggs

6 tbsp - Apple Sauce

1 tsp - Baking Soda

2 tsp - Cream of Tartar

ICING

7 oz. - Raw Coconut Butter (Manna)

Coconut Oil

Raw Honey

DIRECTIONS:

1. Preheat the oven to 375°F. In a large bowl, combine the Chebe flour, cream of tartar, and baking soda. Add the eggs, olive oil, and apple sauce and mix to form dough. Once dough starts to form, use your hands to knead the dough to a smooth consistency. (If dough gets too sticky, add small pinches of Chebe flour to dry it out.)

2. On a sheet of parchment paper, roll the dough into a large square using a rolling pin.

3. In a medium bowl, combine the OMGhee, coconut crystals, tiger nut flour, and cinnamon with a hand mixer. This is the filling. Sprinkle the filling evenly over the large dough square. Tightly roll the dough from one end to the other forming a long tube. Cut the tube into eight individual rolls.

4. Grease the large lidded pan with the 1 tbsp coconut oil and place the rolls evenly inside. Cover the pan with the lid and bake in the oven at 375°F for 20 minutes. After 20 minutes, remove the lid and bake uncovered for another 4-5 minutes.

5. For the icing, slowly heat the coconut manna in the microwave so it gets soft. Stir in 1 tbsp at a time of the raw honey to sweeten the taste. If it starts to get dry, stir in 1 tbsp at a time of coconut oil and pour the icing over the rolls. Separate and serve!

CINNAMON ROLLS

WHAT YOU'LL NEED:

Coconut Oil

3 ½ Cups - Chebe Flour

2 tbsp - Olive Oil

4 - Eggs

6 tbsp - Apple Sauce

1 tsp - Baking Soda

2 tsp - Cream of Tartar

Raw Honey

70% Dark Chocolate Chunks (melted)

DIRECTIONS:

1. In a small pot, melt coconut oil on **MEDIUM/HIGH** so that it fills the pot ¾ of the way up.

2. In a large bowl, combine the dry ingredients. Add the eggs, olive oil, and apple sauce and mix to form dough. Once dough starts to form, use your hand to knead the dough to a smooth consistency. (If dough gets too sticky, add small pinches of Chebe flour to dry it out.)

3. Grab a handful of dough and roll it into a ball. Poke a hole in the center and form it into a donut shape.

4. Drop the donut into the heated coconut oil for 30-60 seconds (depending on the size)

5. Remove the donut with tongs, and let cool. Repeat with the rest of the dough.

6. Glaze with either raw honey or melted 70% dark chocolate chunks.

DONUTS

AIRFRIED ROASTED APPLE

Grain Free   Soy Free   Corn Free

WHAT YOU'LL NEED:

Airfryer heated to 400° F

OMGhee Butter

2 - Apples

Walnut/Pecan Pieces

Raw Honey

Cinnamon

Raisins (optional)

DIRECTIONS:

1. Cut off the tops of the apples making a lid and put aside. With a strong spoon, scoop out the seeds and core, but don't scoop too deep. You don't want to puncture the bottom of the apple.

2. Coat the whole apple (inside and out) with OMGhee Butter.

3. Inside each apple, put a spoonful of raw honey, some nut pieces, a couple sprinkles of cinnamon, and raisins (optional). Place the lids back on top of the apples and bake them in the Airfryer at 400° F for 20 Minutes.

4. Carefully remove the baked apples from the Airfryer with tongs and enjoy. Add more cinnamon as you like.

AIRFRIED ROASTED APPLE

CHIA SEED PUDDING

Grain Free Soy Free Dairy Free Corn Free

WHAT YOU'LL NEED:

Blender

2 cups - Coconut/Almond Milk

½ cup - Coconut Crystals

1 can - Coconut Cream

1 tsp - Vanilla Extract

Pinch of Salt

½ cup - Raw Cacao

¾ cup - Chia Seeds

DIRECTIONS:

1. Place all of the ingredients except for the Chia Seeds in a blender and blend for about 30 seconds on **MEDIUM** to **HIGH** power.

2. Pour the contents into a large bowl and mix in the chia seeds, stirring consistently for 5 minutes.

3. Cover the bowl with plastic wrap or foil and refrigerate for 12 hours, stirring every couple of hours.

4. Divide into containers for serving. Garnish as desired (berries, coconut shavings, nuts, etc.)

CHIA SEED PUDDING

AVOCADO CHOCOLATE PUDDING

Grain Free   Soy Free   Dairy Free   Corn Free

WHAT YOU'LL NEED:

Blender

1 cup - Coconut/Almond Milk

2 - Ripe Avocados

¼ cup + 2 tbsp - Raw Maple Syrup (grade B)

1/3 cup - Cocao Powder

2 tsp - Vanilla Extract

Pinch of Salt

DIRECTIONS:

1. Place all of the ingredients in a blender and blend for about 60 seconds on **MEDIUM** to **HIGH** power.

2. Pour the pudding into a large bowl.

3. Cover the bowl with plastic wrap or foil (or if it has a lid, use that) and refrigerate for 3 hours.

4. Divide into containers for serving. Garnish as desired (berries, coconut shavings, nuts, etc.)

85

AVOCADO CHOCOLATE PUDDING

Made in the USA
Columbia, SC
23 September 2017